LET'S FIND OUT! PRIMARY SOURCES

THE BILL OF RIGHTS

SUSANNA KELLER

Britannica
Educational Publishing

IN ASSOCIATION WITH

ROSEN
EDUCATIONAL SERVICES

Published in 2017 by Britannica Educational Publishing (a trademark of Encyclopædia Britannica, Inc.) in association with The Rosen Publishing Group, Inc.
29 East 21st Street, New York, NY 10010

Distributed exclusively by Rosen Publishing.
To see additional Britannica Educational Publishing titles, go to rosenpublishing.com.

First Edition

Britannica Educational Publishing
J.E. Luebering: Executive Director, Core Editorial
Mary Rose McCudden: Editor, Britannica Student Encyclopedia

Rosen Publishing
Jacob R. Steinberg: Editor
Nelson Sá: Art Director
Nicole Russo: Designer
Cindy Reiman: Photography Manager

Library of Congress Cataloging-in-Publication Data

Names: Keller, Susanna, author.
Title: The Bill of Rights / Susanna Keller.
Description: First edition. | New York : Britannica Educational Publishing in Association with Rosen Educational Services, 2017. | Series: Let's find out! Primary sources | Includes bibliographical references and index. | Audience: Grade 1 to 4.
Identifiers: LCCN 2016025896 | ISBN 9781508103998 (library bound : alk. paper) | ISBN 9781508104001 (pbk. : alk. paper) | ISBN 9781508103219 (6-pack : alk. paper)
Subjects: LCSH: United States. Constitution. 1st–10th Amendments—Juvenile literature. | Constitutional amendments—Juvenile literature. | Civil rights—Juvenile literature.
Classification: LCC KF4750 .K39 2016 | DDC 342.7303—dc23
LC record available at https://lccn.loc.gov/2016025896

Manufactured in China

Photo credits: Cover, p. 1 leezsnow/Getty Images; p. 4 Beinecke Rare Book and Manuscript Library; pp. 5, 11, 28 NARA; p. 6 Bibliotheque Nationale, Paris, France/Bridgeman Images; p. 7 Library of Congress, Washington, D.C.; p. 8 Architect of the Capitol; p. 9 Courtesy National Gallery of Art, Washington, D.C., Alisa Mellon Bruce Fund, 1979.4.2; p. 10 Courtesy National Gallery of Art, Washington, D.C., Gift of Thomas Jefferson Coolidge IV in memory of his great-grandfather, Thomas Jefferson Coolidge, his grandfather, Thomas Jefferson Coolidge II, and his father, Thomas Jefferson Coolidge III, 1986.71; pp. 12, 16, 18, 20, 22, 24, 26 National Archives/The LIFE Picture Collection/Getty Images; p. 13 Sean Pavone/Shutterstock.com; p. 15 Bloomberg/Getty Images; p. 17 Currier & Ives/Library of Congress, Washington, D.C. (LC-USZ62-19); p. 19 © Mikael Karlsson/Alamy Stock Photo; p. 21 Heide Benser/Corbis/Getty Images; p. 23 Andrew Lichtenstein/Corbis News/Getty Images; p. 25 Library of Congress, Washington, D.C. (LC-USZ62-102566); p. 27 Library of Congress, Washington, D.C. (G3710 Ar071300); p. 29 Frederic Lewis/Archive Photos/Getty Images; interior pages background image Tischenko Irina/Shutterstock.com.

CONTENTS

A Primary Source

There are lots of ways to learn about history. One of the best ways is to look at primary sources. These are sources of information that actually come from the time period you want to learn about. Primary sources can be letters, newspaper articles, drawings, photographs, and more. The diary of a Revolutionary War soldier is a primary source, while a history book about the Revolution that was written much later is a secondary source.

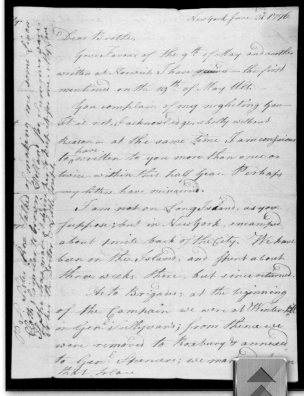

This letter, written by the American patriot Nathan Hale in 1776, is an example of a primary source.

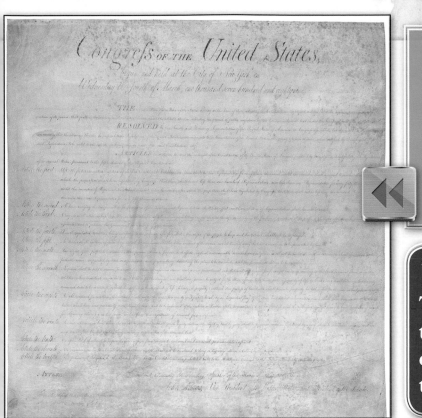

This original handwritten copy of the Bill of Rights is kept in the National Archives in Washington, D.C.

Primary sources help us learn what happened in the past, as well as how people felt about what happened. After all, details get fuzzy as stories are retold. Some of the most studied primary sources are the documents that established the American government. Among the most important of these is the U.S. Bill of Rights. The Bill of Rights is the first ten amendments, or additions, to the **U.S. Constitution**.

Individual Rights

The full title of France's statement of rights is the Declaration of the Rights of Man and of the Citizen.

For much of human history most people did not think of the rights of individual citizens. Rulers often had complete power over the people. One early effort by people to change their government was a document called the Magna Carta (1215). It gave people in England some rights and limited the king's power. Later in history, certain countries created bills of rights. England wrote

THINK ABOUT IT

Which of the statements of individual rights discussed here would you guess had the biggest influence on the U.S. Bill of Rights? Why?

its Bill of Rights in 1689, and France created the Declaration of the Rights of Man in 1789.

As the 13 American colonies considered declaring independence from Great Britain, there was a lot of talk about individual rights. This inspired the state of Virginia to pass a Declaration of Rights on June 12, 1776. The declaration stated that the basis of government was the people. It explained the rights of individuals and set limits on the powers of government.

The Virginia Declaration of Rights was written mostly by the American statesman George Mason.

THE HISTORY OF THE BILL OF RIGHTS

The U.S. Constitution replaced the country's first set of rules, called the Articles of Confederation. There were problems with the Articles so a group of people met in Philadelphia, Pennsylvania, in 1787 to change them. The group soon wrote a completely new document—the Constitution.

One of the problems with the Articles was that the central government was very weak. When the Articles were written, the colonies did not trust a strong government. They were used to the British government making rules that took away their rights.

This 1940 painting, by Howard Chandler Christy, depicts the signing of the U.S. Constitution.

COMPARE AND CONTRAST

Compare the views of the Federalists and the Anti-Federalists. What are the good and bad points of having a strong central government?

However, they soon learned that it was hard to make the states work together with a weak central government.

The Constitution set up a federal system of government. In a federal system the national government and the state governments share power. People who supported this system were called Federalists. Other people were afraid that the new national government would be too strong. They were called Anti-Federalists.

The Constitution did not originally contain a bill of rights. This alarmed the Anti-Federalists. Without such a bill

This 1821 painting shows James Madison, one of the writers of the U.S. Constitution.

they were afraid the national government might take away their newly won freedoms. Thomas Jefferson was one of the men who criticized the new Constitution. In December 1787 he wrote to James Madison, "A bill of rights is what the people are entitled to against every government on earth...and what no just government should refuse or rest on inference."

Thomas Jefferson, seen in this painting from about 1821, was one of the leading Anti-Federalists.

The U.S. Constitution is the oldest written national constitution still in effect today.

As the states **ratified** the Constitution, they did so expecting that a bill of rights would be added to it as soon as the new government was formed. In 1791 the Bill of Rights, containing ten articles written by Madison, was adopted and ratified by the states.

The 1st Amendment

Historians pay close attention to all primary sources. But the text, or words, of the Bill of Rights gets more attention than most primary sources. This is because it is an important part of the U.S. Constitution. It explains

Think About It

Why is it important to spell out the rights of citizens in the Constitution?

Congress shall make no law respecting an establishment of religi

The 1st Amendment guarantees American citizens five important freedoms.

the basic freedoms and rights of all citizens of the United States.

The 1st Amendment protects many rights. It says: "Congress shall make no law respecting an establishment of religion, or prohibiting the free exercise thereof; or abridging the freedom of speech, or of the press; or

The 1st Amendment protects American citizens' right to practice any religion.

the right of the people peaceably to assemble, and to petition the Government for a redress of grievances."

The first part of the amendment says the government cannot pick one religion that everyone has to follow. It also cannot stop people from practicing whatever religion they believe in. The idea that the government should not control, or be controlled by, religion is known as the "separation of church and state."

The amendment also protects freedom of speech—or people's right to express their opinions. This means that the government cannot control what people say. It also means that people will not get in trouble for saying what they think. The amendment also protects freedom of the press. In the 1780s the press was mostly

THINK ABOUT IT

The press provides people with news. What is the advantage of having a press that is not controlled by the government?

newspapers or printed pamphlets, but today it includes television, radio, and the internet.

The last part of the amendment makes sure that people have the right to hold protests or political meetings as long as they are peaceful. It also says that people have the right to complain to the government about any problems in the country.

The right to assemble and protest is also protected by the 1st Amendment.

THE 2ND AMENDMENT

The 2nd Amendment is: "A well regulated Militia, being necessary to the security of a free State, the right of the people to keep and bear Arms, shall not be infringed."

A militia is an organized group of citizens who defend a community. The first battles in the American Revolution were fought by colonial militiamen called minutemen (because they stood ready to fight "at a minute's notice"). The early Americans believed they needed militias to defend their freedom. In fact, clashes with the British over colonial militias sparked the

the right of the people to keep and bear Arms, shall not be infringed

There is a lot of debate about the 2nd Amendment. People disagree about what its meaning is today.

earliest battles in the American Revolution.

The "right to... bear arms" in the 2nd Amendment comes up a lot in discussions about gun control, or limits on owning or carrying guns. Some people think the amendment means that people have the right to own guns for their own self-defense. Other people think the amendment only says that militias have that right.

This illustration shows militiamen heading off to fight the British in the American Revolution.

COMPARE AND CONTRAST

A military is a country's official armed forces. How is it like a militia? How is it different?

THE 3RD AND 4TH AMENDMENTS

The next two amendments protect the rights of people in their own homes. The 3rd Amendment is: "No Soldier shall, in time of peace be quartered in any house, without the consent of the Owner, nor in time of war, but in a manner to be prescribed by law." Before the American Revolution, British soldiers had been quartered, or housed, in the homes of colonists against their will. This was something the Americans complained about in the Declaration of Independence.

against unreasonable searches and seizures

The 4th Amendment protects American citizens "against unreasonable searches and seizures." This is an important protection of privacy.

Thanks to the 4th Amendment, the police need to get a warrant when they search a person's house.

The 4th Amendment protects citizens' "persons, houses, papers, and effects" from "unreasonable searches and seizures." If the police want to search a person's house, they need "probable cause," or good reason to think a crime is being committed. If there is probable cause, they can get a **warrant** "describing the place to be searched, and the persons or things to be seized." Probable cause is also needed to arrest a person.

VOCABULARY

A **warrant** is a legal paper giving an officer the power to carry out the law.

THE 5TH AMENDMENT

The 5th Amendment states that a person cannot be tried for certain serious crimes without "indictment of a Grand Jury." An indictment is an official statement of the crime a person is accused of. This amendment also protects a person from being tried more than once for the same crime.

It also states that a person cannot "be compelled in any criminal case to be a witness against himself." This means people accused of crimes do not have to speak at their trial if doing so might help make them be found guilty.

...be deprived of life, liberty, or property, without due process of law

The 5th Amendment protects people who are on trial after having been accused of a crime.

Choosing not to speak at your own trial is called "pleading the fifth" after the 5th Amendment.

A person cannot be "deprived of life, liberty, or property, without due process of law" (that is, a legal process that protects a person's rights) thanks to the 5th Amendment. It also says that the government cannot take a person's property without "just compensation," or fair payment.

COMPARE AND CONTRAST

The 5th Amendment guarantees several rights. What do these rights have in common? How are each different?

THE 6TH, 7TH, AND 8TH AMENDMENTS

The next three amendments also deal with the rights of people on trial. The 6th Amendment promises a "speedy and public trial, by an impartial jury of the State and district wherein the crime shall have been committed." Trials cannot be secret or delayed. Furthermore, they must happen in the same place as the crime occurred.

hall enjoy the right to a speedy and public trial,

The Bill of Rights guarantees important rights for Americans who have been accused of crimes.

The 7th Amendment requires a trial before a jury for certain civil cases. It says that the decisions on these cases cannot be overturned. Civil cases involve disagreements between two people, often over money.

"Excessive bail shall not be required, nor excessive fines imposed, nor cruel and unusual punishments inflicted," according to the 8th Amendment. Bail is the deposit of money needed to temporarily free a prisoner. The "cruel and unusual punishments" part makes sure that prisoners will not be treated too harshly.

THINK ABOUT IT

Some people argue that sentencing people to death is a "cruel and unusual punishment." What do you think?

These people are protesting against the practice of sentencing people to death for their crimes.

23

THE 9TH AMENDMENT

The 9th Amendment is: "The enumeration in the Constitution, of certain rights, shall not be construed to deny or disparage others retained by the people." This means that people are not limited to only the rights clearly listed in the Constitution.

This amendment made it into the Bill of Rights because of the debate between the Federalists and the Anti-Federalists over ratifying the Constitution. Anti-Federalists wanted the Bill of Rights so that the federal

The enumeration in the Constitution, of certain rights, shall not be construed to deny or disparage others retained by the people.

The 9th Amendment makes it clear that the rights American citizens have are not limited to only those listed in the Constitution.

Patrick Henry was one of the people who worried that the Constitution would not protect individual rights.

government would not have too much power and individuals' rights would be protected. The Federalists replied that spelling out which individual rights were protected might make people think that any rights not listed were not protected. The 9th Amendment was added to make it clear that this is not the case.

COMPARE AND CONTRAST

The Federalists and the Anti-Federalists both helped shape the Bill of Rights. How were their concerns different? What concerns do you think they shared?

THE 10TH AMENDMENT

The last of the amendments in the Bill of Rights states that, "The powers not delegated to the United States by the Constitution, nor prohibited by it to the States, are reserved to the States respectively, or to the people." This means that any powers that are not mentioned as belonging to the federal government in the Constitution belong to the people and the states.

Like the amendment before it, the 10th Amendment was added because of the disagreements between the Federalists and Anti-Federalists. The Anti-Federalists

reserved to the States respectively, or to the people.

The 10th Amendment supports the division of power between the central government and the governments of the individual states.

COMPARE AND CONTRAST

The 10th Amendment deals with powers while the 9th deals with rights. How are rights and powers similar? How are they different?

worried that the Constitution gave the federal government too much power over the states and citizens. This amendment helps maintain the separation of powers. Power is spread around to different levels and branches of government, so none can become too powerful.

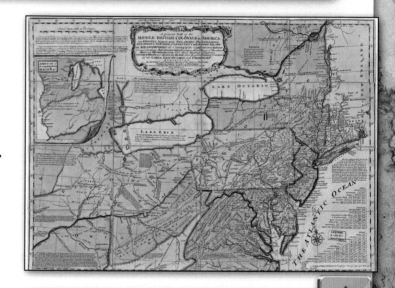

This map from 1758 shows some of the thirteen British colonies that would later become the first U.S. states.

THE BILL OF RIGHTS TODAY

The Bill of Rights contained the first ten amendments to the U.S. Constitution. These would not be the only amendments to be added, though. One of the most important later amendments was the 14th, which gave all Americans "equal protection of the laws." The 15th Amendment gave African American men the right to vote, while the 19th gave women the right to vote as well. Amendments can still be

The 14th Amendment granted American citizenship to former slaves.

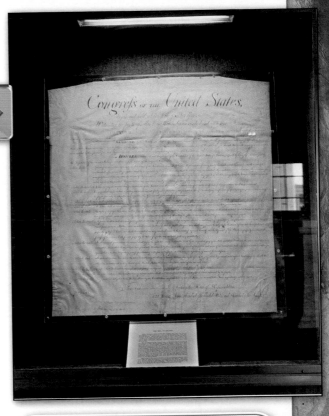

Copies of the Bill of Rights were made for each of the original thirteen states.

added, and people still suggest them today.

The amendments that are already part of the Constitution continue to be important, too. People look to them to see if laws are constitutional. They use them to argue that other laws are not. Arguments over prayer in schools, gun control, and the rights of groups of people all depend on the first ten amendments. The Bill of Rights continues to be central to American democracy.

THINK ABOUT IT

The Bill of Rights has ten amendments. Which one do you think is the most important? Why?

GLOSSARY

amendment A change or addition to something, especially a law.

citizen A full member of a country, who is protected by its laws.

delegate A person sent with power to act for another.

democracy Government in which the supreme power is held by the people.

document A written or printed paper giving information about or proof of something.

guarantee To promise something.

indictment An official charge that a person committed a crime.

inflict To cause something, often something painful, to happen.

interpret To explain the meaning (of something).

jury A body of persons sworn to inquire into a matter of fact and give their verdict.

militia A body of citizens with some military training who are called to active duty only in an emergency.

prohibit To order something not to be done.

represent To act in the place of another.

sentence To impose a judgment on another.

trial The hearing and judgment of a case in court.

unconstitutional Not in agreement with the Constitution.

FOR MORE INFORMATION

Books

Baxter, Roberta. *The Bill of Rights* (Documenting U.S. History). Chicago, IL: Heinemann Library, 2013.

Clay, Kathryn. *The U.S. Constitution* (Smithsonian Little Explorer). North Mankato, MN: Capstone Press, 2016.

Krull, Kathleen. *A Kids' Guide to America's Bill of Rights*. Revised edition. New York, NY: Harper Collins, 2015.

Maloof, Torrey. *We the People: Founding Documents* (Primary Source Readers). Huntington Beach, CA: Teacher Created Materials, 2016.

Raatma, Lucia. *The Bill of Rights* (Cornerstones of Freedom). New York, NY: Children's Press, 2012.

Websites

Because of the changing nature of internet links, Rosen Publishing has developed an online list of websites related to the subject of this book. This site is updated regularly. Please use this link to access the list:

http://www.rosenlinks.com/LFO/bill

INDEX